HOW TO DRAW FANTASY ART

Mark Bergin

PowerKiDS press.

New York

Published in 2011 by The Rosen Publishing Group, Inc.
29 East 21st Street, New York, NY 10010

Editor: Rob Walker
U.S. Editor: Kara Murray

Library of Congress Cataloging-in-Publication Data

Bergin, Mark.
  How to draw fantasy art / Mark Bergin. — 1st ed.
      p. cm. — (How to draw)
  Includes index.
  ISBN 978-1-4488-1578-4 (library binding) — ISBN 978-1-4488-1601-9 (pbk.) —
ISBN 978-1-4488-1602-6 (6-pack)
  1. Fantasy in art—Juvenile literature. 2. Drawing—Technique—
Juvenile literature. I. Title.
  NC825.F25B47 2011
  743'.87—dc22

                                  2010002558

Manufactured in Heshan, China

CPSIA Compliance Information: Batch #SS0102PK:
For Further Information contact Rosen Publishing, New York, New York at 1-800-237-9932

Contents

Making a Start

Learning to draw is about looking and seeing. Keep practicing, and get to know your subject. Use a sketchbook to make quick drawings. Start by doodling, and experiment with shapes and patterns. There are many ways to draw. This book shows just one method. Visit art galleries, look at artists' drawings, see how friends draw, but above all, find your own way.

Remember that practice makes
perfect. If it looks wrong, start again.
Keep working at it, The more you
draw, the more you will learn.

Perspective

If you look at any object from different viewpoints, you will see that the part that is closest to you looks larger and the part farthest away from you looks smaller. Drawing in perspective is a way of creating a feeling of depth, or of showing three dimensions on a flat surface.

The vanishing point (V.P.) is the place in a perspective drawing where parallel lines appear to meet. The position of the vanishing point depends on the viewer's eye level. Sometimes a low viewpoint can give your drawing added drama.

V.P.

V.P.

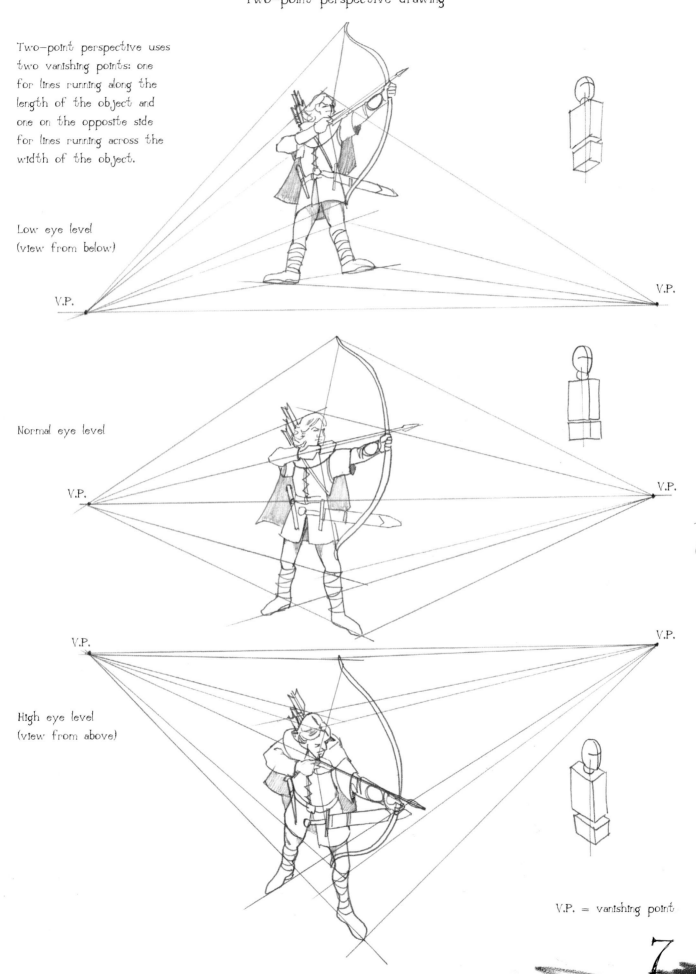

Two-point perspective uses two vanishing points: one for lines running along the length of the object and one on the opposite side for lines running across the width of the object.

Low eye level
(view from below)

V.P.   V.P.

Normal eye level

V.P.   V.P.

V.P.   V.P.

High eye level
(view from above)

V.P. = vanishing point

7

Drawing Materials

Try using different types of drawing papers and materials. Experiment with charcoal, wax crayons, and pastels. All pens, from felt-tips to ballpoints, will make interesting marks, or try drawing with pen and ink on wet paper.

Pastels are even softer than charcoal and come in a wide range of colors. Ask an adult to spray your pastel drawings with fixative to prevent smudging.

Silhouette is a style of drawing that uses only a solid black shadow.

You can create special effects by scraping away parts of a drawing done with **wax crayons.**

Felt-tips

8

Pencils

Hard **pencils** are grayer and soft pencils are blacker. Pencils are graded from #1 (the softest) to #4 (the hardest).

Pen and ink

Charcoal is very soft and can be used for big, bold drawings. Ask an adult to spray your charcoal drawings with fixative to prevent smudging.

Lines drawn in **ink** cannot be erased, so keep your ink drawings sketchy and less rigid. Don't worry about mistakes as these lines can be lost in the drawing as it develops.

Character Proportions

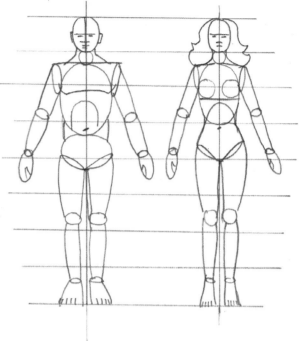

This page shows some of the more popular fantasy figures and their proportions compared to a normal human figure. On average, the length of a human head should fit eight times into its body length. When you draw a fantasy figure, anything goes, so let your imagination go wild.

Draw these simple figures to help you choose a good position for your character. You can emphasize the qualities of a character by using dramatic poses or emotions.

Man Beasts

Combining a human figure with an animal's head can create a great hybrid monster. You can get inspiration by drawing from life models. Photos from sports movies and figure reference manuals are a good source too. Why not try putting a snake or insect's head on a human body? See what you can create!

The Minotaur is half bull and half man.

Werewolf: a human that takes on the shape of a wolf when there is a full moon.

Dragonman: the body of a man with the characteristics of a dragon added.

Amazon Warrior

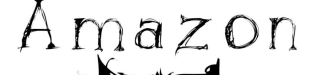

This powerful female figure is a classic action fantasy character. She must look strong and powerful but retain her femininity and beauty.

Draw ovals for the head, neck, body, and hips.

Draw a long, curved line to start the position of the body.

Add the basic shape of the hand.

Sketch cylinder shapes for each arm that join at the elbow.

Legs: add the curved lines of the upper and lower leg, indicating the knee joint.

Add the foot shape and direction.

Drawing Hands

Practice sketching your own hands in different positions. This will help you draw expressive hands on your characters.

Add the sword using straight lines.

Sketch the position of the ears, nose, and mouth.

Sketch the shape of the hair mass.

Indicate the position and shape of the chest.

Add the costume's draped cloth using simple lines.

Finish the detail on the sword. Small broken lines give the impression of shining metal.

Add fingers to each hand.

Add tone and details to the hair.

Draw the top of the costume.

Add shade to areas where the light would not reach.

Draw the boot shapes.

Draw bracelets and armbands.

Add tone to the legs.

Complete the details on the boots.

Remove any unwanted construction lines.

15

Warrior Queen

This character's commanding stance oozes strength and power but still displays her femininity through her flowing cloak and costume. Her sword displays the metal-working skills of the elves, the great sword masters.

Draw ovals for the head, neck, body, and hips.

Draw in a center line.

Add cylinder shapes for each arm, showing elbow joints.

Draw in the basic shape of the hands.

Draw straight lines for the legs. Indicate knee joints.

Draw in the basic shape and direction of the feet.

Mark the position of the eyes, nose, and mouth.

Draw the position of the fingers.

Draw in the position and shape of the chest.

Draw in the belt, making sure it goes around the figure.

Sketch in the shape of the sword.

Character Concepts

Using the same basic head shape, you can create your own variety of character heads, from monster to female to Orc!

Add more detail to the face.

Sketch in the hood raised over the head.

Draw in the shape of the cloak with long, curved lines.

Draw the fingers of the hand.

Add the shape of the bodice and sleeves.

Add shading under the hood and add the headband.

Using flowing lines draw in the hair.

Draw in arm guards.

Add decorative details to the sword.

Use straight lines to indicate the folds in the fabric.

Shade areas where the light will not reach.

Remove any unwanted construction lines.

Finish details on the feet.

Add shadows under the hem of the dress.

17

Barbarian

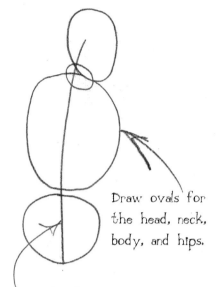

This fierce northern warrior comes from feudal warmongering tribes. He has an impressive muscular build with broad shoulders and large, powerful arms as he relies on his strength in combat. His weapons are heavy and oversized to inflict the maximum damage to his opponents.

Draw ovals for the head, neck, body, and hips.

Draw a center line.

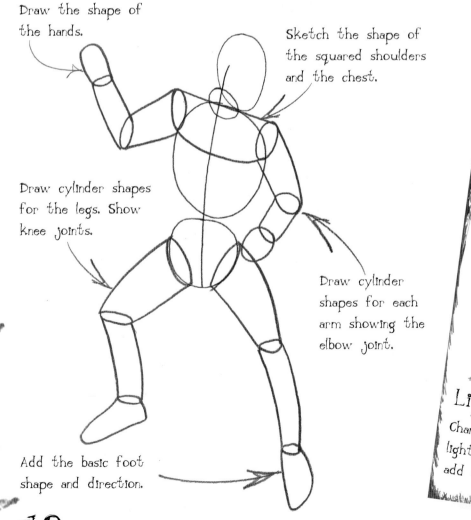

Draw the shape of the hands.

Sketch the shape of the squared shoulders and the chest.

Draw cylinder shapes for the legs. Show knee joints.

Draw cylinder shapes for each arm showing the elbow joint.

Add the basic foot shape and direction.

Light from above

Light from above at a diagonal angle

Light from the side

Light from below

Light

Changing the direction of the light source in a drawing can add drama and mood.

Draw the shape of the fingers.

Add the horned helmet using curved lines.

Sketch the position of the eyes, nose, and mouth.

Draw long, curved lines to show the shape of the cape.

Draw the sword, scabbard, and belt.

Draw the ax heads, embellishing them with details.

Draw in both the axe shafts.

Add the details of the face, the hair, and helmet.

Sketch the tops of the boots.

Draw decorative wrist guards.

Use curved lines to add muscles to the body.

Draw the loincloth.

Add tone to the legs.

Finish the detail on the boots.

Remove any unwanted construction lines.

Shade areas where light would not reach, especially to the inside folds of the cloak.

19

Ogre

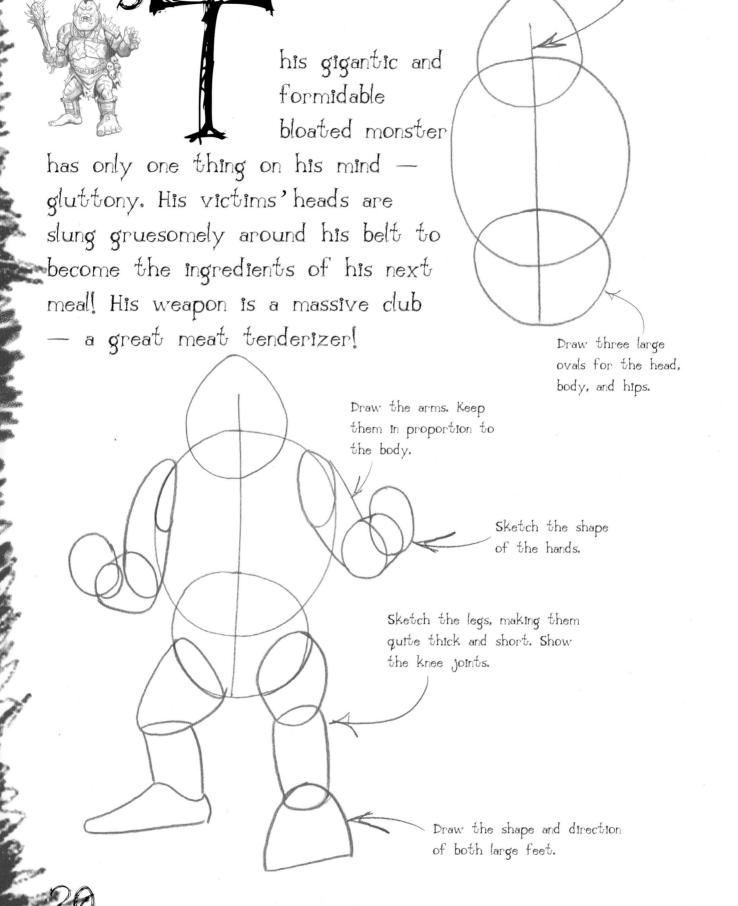

This gigantic and formidable bloated monster has only one thing on his mind — gluttony. His victims' heads are slung gruesomely around his belt to become the ingredients of his next meal! His weapon is a massive club — a great meat tenderizer!

Draw a center line for the figure.

Draw three large ovals for the head, body, and hips.

Draw the arms. Keep them in proportion to the body.

Sketch the shape of the hands.

Sketch the legs, making them quite thick and short. Show the knee joints.

Draw the shape and direction of both large feet.

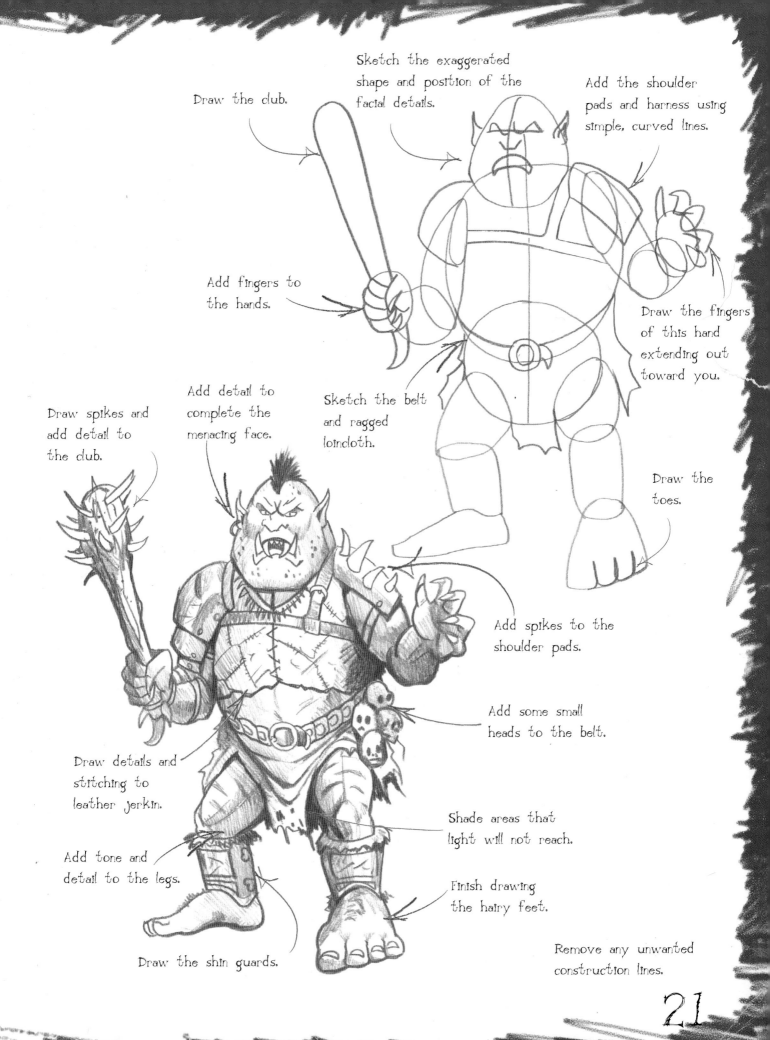

Draw the club.

Sketch the exaggerated shape and position of the facial details.

Add the shoulder pads and harness using simple, curved lines.

Add fingers to the hands.

Draw the fingers of this hand extending out toward you.

Draw spikes and add detail to the club.

Add detail to complete the menacing face.

Sketch the belt and ragged loincloth.

Add spikes to the shoulder pads.

Draw the toes.

Add some small heads to the belt.

Draw details and stitching to leather jerkin.

Shade areas that light will not reach.

Add tone and detail to the legs.

Finish drawing the hairy feet.

Draw the shin guards.

Remove any unwanted construction lines.

21

Undead Warrior

This once proud warrior has turned, in death, into a hideous and terrifying evil demon. His head is reduced to a skull and flesh hangs from his body. He is summoned up to collect the souls of dead warriors on the battlefield.

Draw ovals for the head, neck, body, and hips.

Draw a center line.

Sketch the shape and position of the arms with cylinder shapes. Show elbow joints.

Add basic shapes for the hands.

Sketch the legs, showing the knee joints.

Draw the feet pointing down.

Action Poses

Draw lots of small figures to find the best pose. Try out poses yourself in front of a mirror to see what looks good.

Draw the sword using long, curved lines for the blade.

Sketch the head details: the facial structure and the helmet.

Draw circles for the shield.

Draw the scabbard, sword, and belt.

Draw a small ax tucked in the belt.

Sketch the start of the bandages on the legs.

Add detail to the face and helmet.

Add detail to the armor.

Make the sword look shiny by drawing straight lines across the length of the sword.

Add the details of the body.

Add gruesome detail to the legs: bones showing through the flesh.

Add detail and tone to the shield.

Shade areas that light will not reach.

Finish drawing the bandages around the legs.

Remove any unwanted construction lines.

23

Winged Avenger

T his dynamic female angel hunts out evil on her wings. Her wings are her most powerful limbs. She uses magic weapons and a shield to protect and defend herself against the evil forces that fight against her.

Draw ovals for the head, neck, body, and hips.

Sketch a center line that continues through the extended leg.

Draw cylinder shapes for the arms, showing the elbow joints.

Sketch the basic shape of the hands.

Sketch the positions of the facial features.

Indicate the position and shape of the chest.

Sketch the position of the raised leg and foot.

Add the trailing leg and foot using the center line as a guide.

Add curved lines to the torso, dividing up each section of clothing and body.

Sketch the position of the wings using long, curved lines.

Add more facial details.

Draw the shape of the shield.

Draw the weapon clasped in her hand.

Sketch shape of the trailing leg.

Draw wing features using carefully curved lines.

Draw the flowing hair.

Shade areas that light will not reach.

Add detail and tone to the shield.

Complete all details on the torso and costume.

Add flowing drapery.

Add all finishing details to the boots.

Remove any unwanted construction lines.

25

War Wizard

The war wizard's well-honed physique gives him his strength. Magic powers that flow through his fingertips strike down his enemies. The heads of his evil opponents hang from his belt as trophies, ready to be made into potions later.

Add ovals for the head, neck, body, and hips.

Draw a center line.

Draw two straight lines from the middle of the bottom oval.

Lightly sketch two curved lines on the face to help position its features.

Sketch the arms using cylinder shapes. Indicate elbow joints.

Draw the basic shape of the hands.

Use cylinder shapes to sketch in the position of the legs.

Add the shape and direction of the feet.

Facial Expressions

Puzzled   Annoyed   Sad   Shocked

Sinister   Mischievous   Gritted teeth   Joy

Experiment with different facial expressions for your character depending on his situation. Make different faces in front of a mirror to get an idea of how to depict emotions.

26

Draw the hand details with a finger pointed up.

Add in the basic shape of the hair mass and the beard.

Sketch the positions of the eyes, nose, and mouth.

Draw jagged lines around the hand to show his magic powers.

Sketch the sword and belt.

Draw the wizard's staff.

Draw in all the facial details.

Use curved lines to add detail to the wizard's hair.

Draw remaining details of the torso.

Add head trophies to his belt.

Add detail to the staff and sword.

Draw the wizard's robe using long, curved lines.

Complete the robe using tone to show folds. Add jagged lines to show the tattered edges.

Draw the wizard's boots.

Add shading to areas that light does not reach, particularly to the inside of the robe.

Remove any unwanted construction lines.

27

Goblin

This evil and devious creature is a fierce fighter. He will be found in dark mountain areas where great goblin armies scheme and plan their battles against the dwarf lords. They are not the strongest opponents, but they overwhelm their enemies with their great numbers.

Draw a center line with another crossing it.

Add the position of the neck.

Draw three ovals for the head, body, and hips.

Sketch the position of the facial features.

Add pointed ears.

Draw a long straight line for the spear shaft.

Sketch three ovals for shoulders and arms.

Draw curved lines for the shape of the legs.

Draw two oval shapes for the shape of the hand.

Sketch circles for the knees and ankles.

Draw the shape and direction of the feet.

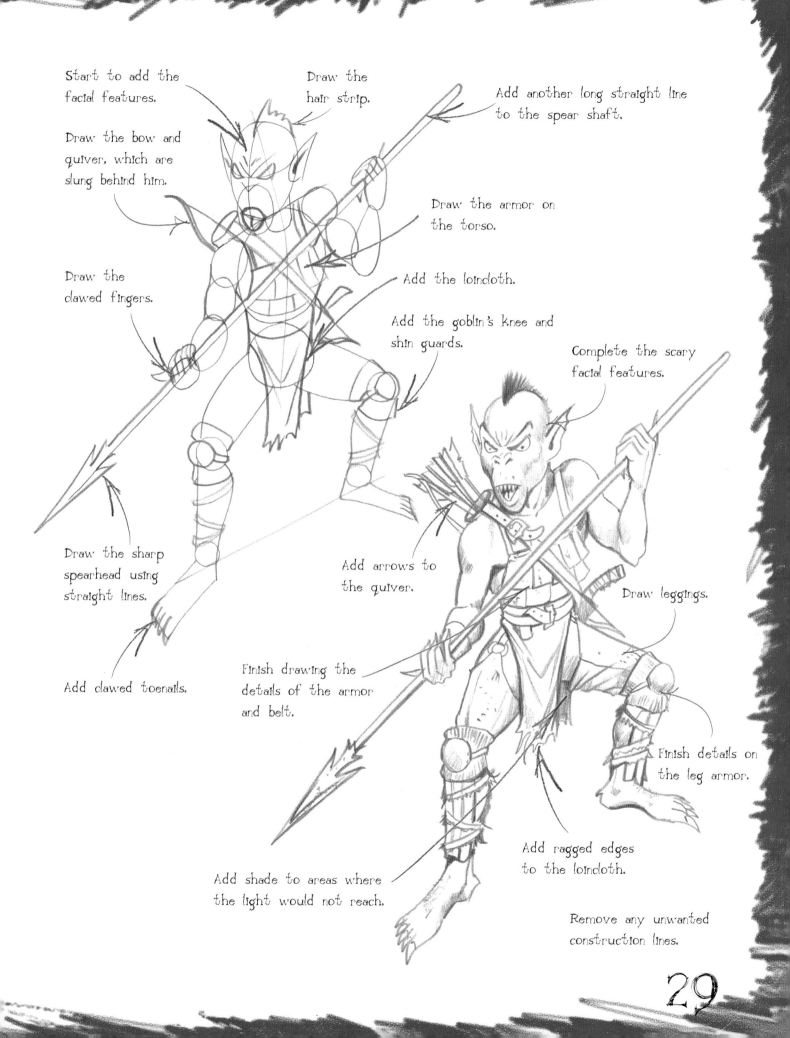

Start to add the facial features.

Draw the hair strip.

Add another long straight line to the spear shaft.

Draw the bow and quiver, which are slung behind him.

Draw the armor on the torso.

Complete the scary facial features.

Draw the clawed fingers.

Add the loincloth.

Add the goblin's knee and shin guards.

Draw the sharp spearhead using straight lines.

Add arrows to the quiver.

Draw leggings.

Finish drawing the details of the armor and belt.

Finish details on the leg armor.

Add clawed toenails.

Add ragged edges to the loincloth.

Add shade to areas where the light would not reach.

Remove any unwanted construction lines.

Goblin vs. Warrior

Draw this action fighting scene: the crouching goblin is ready to strike at the upright stance of the brave, defending warrior who towers over him. Always remember to sketch in your initial drawing lightly so that you can add in more detail later.

Draw a center line for each figure.

Sketch ovals for the head, neck, body, and hips of each figure.

Draw the basic shape of the hands.

Sketch a straight line for the position of the shoulders.

Draw the arms of each figure using simple cylinder shapes.

Draw the shape and direction of each foot.

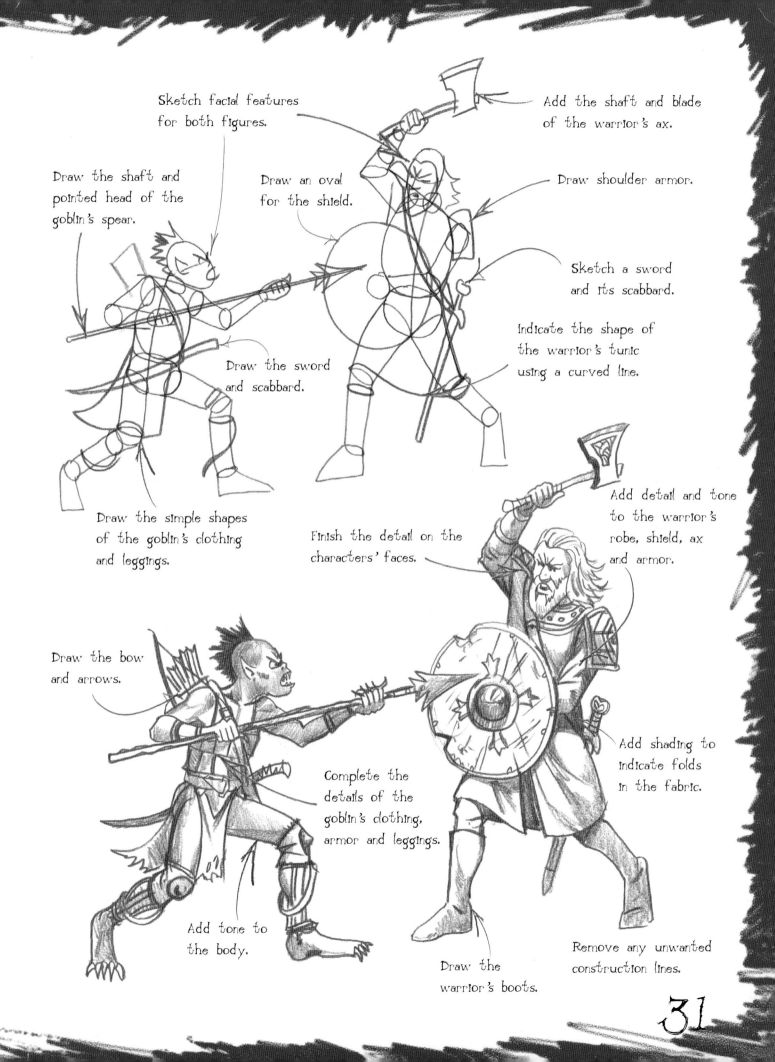

Sketch facial features for both figures.

Add the shaft and blade of the warrior's ax.

Draw the shaft and pointed head of the goblin's spear.

Draw an oval for the shield.

Draw shoulder armor.

Sketch a sword and its scabbard.

Draw the sword and scabbard.

Indicate the shape of the warrior's tunic using a curved line.

Draw the simple shapes of the goblin's clothing and leggings.

Finish the detail on the characters' faces.

Add detail and tone to the warrior's robe, shield, ax and armor.

Draw the bow and arrows.

Complete the details of the goblin's clothing, armor and leggings.

Add shading to indicate folds in the fabric.

Add tone to the body.

Draw the warrior's boots.

Remove any unwanted construction lines.

31

Glossary

center line (SEN–tur LYN) Often used as the starting point of the drawing, it marks the middle of the object or figure.

construction lines (kun–STRUK–shun LYNZ) Guidelines used in the early stages of a drawing, and usually erased later.

fixative (FIK–suh–tiv) A type of resin used to spray over a finished drawing to prevent smudging. **It should be used only by an adult.**

light source (LYT SAWRS) The direction from which the light seems to come in a drawing.

perspective (per–SPEK–tiv) A method of drawing in which near objects are shown larger than faraway objects to give an impression of depth.

pose (POHZ) The position assumed by a figure.

proportion (pruh–POR–shun) The correct relationship of scale between each part of a drawing.

silhouette (sih–luh–WET) A drawing that shows only a flat dark shape, like a shadow.

sketchbook (SKECH–buhk) A book for making quick drawings.

vanishing point (VA–nish–ing POYNT) The place in a perspective drawing where parallel lines appear to meet.

Index

Web Sites

Due to the changing nature of Internet links, PowerKids Press has developed an online list of Web sites related to the subject of this book. This site is updated regularly. Please use this link to access the list:

www.powerkidslinks.com/howtodraw/fantasy/